D0593694

Stangl and Pennsbury Birds

An Identification and Price guide

Mike Schneider

77 Lower Valley Road, Atglen, PA 19310

Dedication

To Cindy, whom I met a decade and a half before the Stangl Pottery closed, and who, like the birds in this book, has remained just as beautiful and become more appreciated with each passing year.

3400 Lovebird (original)
3404D Lovebirds (original)

These are the original lovebirds, as opposed to the revised lovebirds which are shown on page 28. Height of the single bird is 4 inches; the revised one is slightly taller. The pair stands 4 7/8 inches high. Like the single, the original pair is a tad shorter than the revised pair, but the main difference is that this pair is actually kissing, the revised pair is not. They are also shown on page 28. Estimated value: $55 single, $130 double.

Copyright © 1994 by Mike Schneider
Library of Congress Catalog Number: 94-65630

All rights reserved. No part of this work may be reproduced or used in any forms or by any means –graphic, electronic or mechanical, including photocopying or information storage and retrieval systems–without written permission from the copyright holder.

Printed in Hong Kong.
ISBN: 0-88740-612-2

Published by Schiffer Publishing, Ltd.
77 Lower Valley Road
Atglen, PA 19310
Please write for a free catalog.
This book may be purchased from the publisher.
Please include $2.95 postage.
Try your bookstore first.

We are interested in hearing from authors with book ideas on related subjects.

Contents

3406 Kingfisher

The kingfisher was made in both blue and green, the green version appearing on 38. This figure is 3 3/4 inches high. Estimated value: blue $50, green $75.

The double bluejays shown on the title page make up one of the premiere pieces in the Stangl Birds of America series. No. 3717D, this figure could serve as the focal point of just about any Stangl collection. It is shown from a different angle on page 86.

Acknowledgments

The four collectors who contributed to this work requested anonymity. I want them to know that I sincerely appreciate and thank them for the time and energy they put into helping me complete it.

As always my wife, Cindy, helped in many ways. Perhaps her greatest contribution over the years has been her unwavering support of every writing project I have undertaken.

I would also like to thank Peter Schiffer, president of Schiffer Publishing Ltd, for trusting my judgement concerning the subject matter of this and all my books.

Most importantly, I want to thank you, the reader, for your interest in collecting. Without it I would have little about which to write.

3584 Large Cockatoo

Stangl made three sizes of cockatoos, small, medium and large, plus a small double cockatoo. This large example, finished in antique gold, is 12 3/8 inches high. Estimated value: $175.

Introduction

This is a simple book with a simple premise: to provide collectors a photo album of individual color pictures of Stangl birds, and to eliminate the confusion that often exists between those birds and the very similar ones that were made by the Pennsbury Pottery. It shows all of Stangl's Birds of America series but one, the single white-winged crossbill. This should not cause too much of a problem as the single white-winged crossbill looks very much like the double white-winged crossbill, which is shown. Estimated values are also provided. The Stangl birds are shown in numerical order according to the numbers on their bottoms. If you wish to look up a Stangl bird by name instead of number, consult the Stangl Index at the back of the book.

3582D Double Parakeets

The double parakeets were made in green as shown here, and also in blue-green as shown on page 68. Height is 7 1/2 inches. Estimated value: $200.

For those who desire an in-depth study of the Stangl Pottery and its various wares, I highly recommend the excellent book, *Stangl Pottery*, by Harvey Duke (Wallace-Homestead Book Company, 1993). It goes light years beyond the scope of this elementary identification and price guide. The Duke book gives a thorough history of the pottery. It also pictures, describes and prices numerous other Stangl lines in addition to the birds.

The Pennsbury birds, which are fewer in number than the Stangls, appear in a separate section but in no particular order. Like the Stangls, each is assigned an estimated value. There is also a separate Pennsbury Index in the back of the book.

If you wish to learn more about Pennsbury Pottery and its many lines, the best reference is *Pennsbury Pottery*, by Lucille Henzke (Schiffer, 1990). An all color book with more than 500 photos, it displays not only the birds but virtually all of Pennsbury's output including the very popular Amish, Red Rooster and Black Rooster lines. Information on how to obtain both books can be found in Appendix 1: Sources.

To aid collectors who wish to go beyond that, the bibliography lists all the Stangl and Pennsbury information I reviewed while writing this book. I would warn readers, however, that many of the early articles about Stangl birds are laced with misinformation, and that the Duke book provides the most accurate record to date of the Stangl Pottery, its history and products.

Another good source of information is the Stangl Bird Collectors' Association, which was organized in 1992. Its membership numbers in the hundreds. It has annual meeting each spring and sponsors an art pottery show each fall. A newsletter is published four times per year. Information on how to join is listed in Appendix 1: Sources.

3405 Cockatoo (small)

The small cockatoo is 6 1/8" high. This one has a lighter glaze than the standard version on page 35. Because of that it is sometimes called the white cockatoo. Estimated value: $50.

Chapter 1:
Stangl History

J. Martin Stangl, the owner of the Stangl Pottery, was a German-born, German-educated ceramic engineer. In 1910, at the age of 22, he went to work as plant superintendent at the Fulper Pottery, in Flemington, New Jersey. Fulper was originally a drain tile pottery, started in the early 1800s by a man named Samuel Hill. A couple years after his death in 1858 an employee named Abraham Fulper, said to be a relative of Hill's, purchased the plant. Over the years it was passed down through the Fulper family and, by the time Stangl arrived, it had expanded its lines to include not only utilitarian ware, but art ware, too.

Stangl's first association with Fulper was rather short. The young immigrant left in 1914 for a position with the Haeger Potteries, of Dundee, Illinois. But he returned to Fulper in 1920 to serve as general manager, and ten years later bought the company lock, stock and kilns. A year earlier, in 1929, a fire had destroyed the Flemington plant. Rather than rebuild, the company switched all manufacturing to a plant in

3456 Cerulean Warbler

This is a gilted version of the Cerulean warbler. It is 3 7/8 inches high. It appears in its natural colors on page 60. Although some collectors make distinctions, most Stangl birds that were finished differently than the norm sell for around the same price as those that received standard colors. Estimated value: $55.

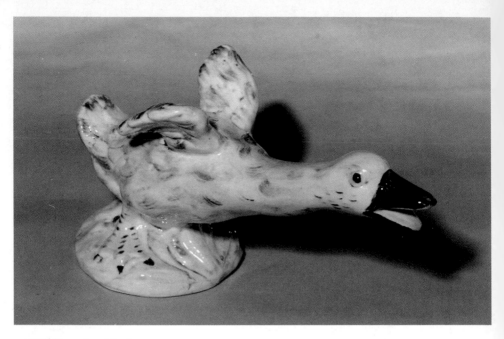

3432 Running Duck

A running duck finished in what Duke refers to as grayish white with black spots. It is 5 1/4 inches high. The natural version is shown on page 41. Estimated value: $475.

Trenton, about 15 miles away, that it had acquired a few years earlier. A small building spared from the 1929 fire was then enlarged to serve as a research and development facility, warehouse, outlet store and, at times, a decorating studio.

Stangl birds made their debut in 1940. And although they were marketed from 1940 to 1978, many collectors divide them into two groups, those sold from 1940 through 1972, and those sold between 1974 and 1978. That's because J. Martin Stangl died early in 1972 and the company was purchased a few months later by new owners who resumed production of the birds in 1974.

These later birds were made from the original molds but used a different numbering system. Some were dated, some were made of a terra cotta earthenware instead of the white earthenware used previously.

All operations at the Stangl Pottery ceased in 1978 when its buildings were bought by the Pfaltzgraff Pottery Company, which shut it down permanently almost before the ink was dry on the purchase agreement.

Stangl bird figurines are loosely based on John J. Audubon's *Birds of America*, first published in four parts between 1827 and 1838, and re-

Stangl Dealer's Sign

One of the really hard Stangl bird items to find is the dealer's sign. It measures
5 3/8 x 6 inches. Estimated value: $1000.

printed in one form or another countless times since. The term "loosely
based" is used because, while Audubon's bird paintings were lifelike in
every detail, Stangl's bird figurines are clearly decorative. Stangl birds
were made with much more vivid colors than those used by Audubon,
whose paintings were about as close to a photograph as you could get
in those days when there was no such thing as a photograph. Because
Stangl birds were handpainted instead of airbrushed, changes from one
color to another are abrupt, not subtle as in nature or the Audubon
prints. And finally, Stangl made a number of birds that Audubon never
painted. Two that come to mind right away are the ringneck pheasant,
an Asiatic import that was not introduced in the United States until
long after the artist's 1851 death, and the penguin which has never established a wild population on the North American continent.

One more thing that must be mentioned is the porcelain birds. In
the early 1940s Stangl conducted a brief experiment with a more highly
detailed and very expensive line of porcelain birds. While it resulted in
failure then, today the porcelain birds are some of the rarest and most
highly sought of Stangl's many products. They are covered more thor-
oughly in Appendix 2: Stangl Porcelain Birds.

Chapter 2:
Stangl Marks

Stangl birds are marked in various ways, most of which are shown below. Some carry an impressed mark. Others have an incised one. Model numbers, especially, were often incised. Inkstamps, paper labels, paper hang tags and, occasionally, hand marking by decorators were also used. As you can see below, many Stangl birds were marked with a combination of two or more of these methods. Rare indeed is the Stangl bird that has no mark.

According to nearly all sources, the name change from Fulper Pottery to Stangl Pottery wasn't officially made until 1955, fully a quarter century after Stangl purchased it. Marks, however, reflected the change of ownership almost immediately. Most of the time when you encounter an impressed Fulper mark, such as that on the flying duck shown below, the term Fulper artware would describe it more appropriately than the term Stangl bird.

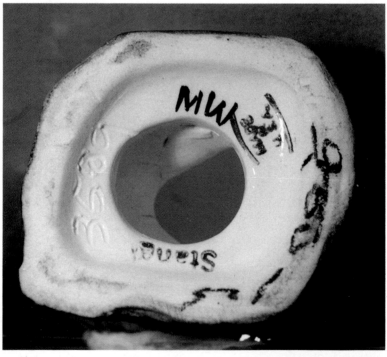

The bottom of the indigo bunting shown on page 72. The smeared part of the mark reads "Made / in / U.S.A." on three lines. MW is the decorator's initials. Look closely and you might be able to see the incised model number, 3589. The one time seller's grease pencil marks numerically define the word inflation.

A blue mark instead of brown on the paroquet (parrot) that is shown on page 52. Note, too, that the model number is stamped instead of incised.

Paper labels are apparently a different matter, considering that the Fulper label shown below was found on the double Audubon warblers, which were clearly part of the Stangl Birds of America line. The hang tags that originally accompanied each bird displayed both names, Stangl on one side, Fulper on the other.

While not every mark Stangl used on its birds appears below, those that are shown are typical of the large majority you will find.

Every so often, however, you will find a bird that is not marked. For the most part these are seconds that were sold early on through the company's factory outlet store before it began marking its irregulars. But the possibility exists, too, that they may have been oversights by employees whose minds were on something other than work on any particular day. Unmarked birds present little problem to collectors if they have been finished in standard colors and style.

Identification of non-standard pieces is a bit more perplexing. According to Duke, Stangl seldom pitched anything in the trash. His research revealed that seconds were sometimes decorated in other than normal colors, then sold at reduced prices at the outlet store. Also, if Stangl followed the pattern of most other potteries, and there is no reason to believe it didn't, the outlet store would have been used in part to gauge public reaction to new or altered items prior to putting them into full production, a sort of close-to-home test marketing procedure. Then, too, there are the so called "lunch hour" pieces, items that were made in nonstandard color schemes for an employee's own use. The result of these three circumstances is that birds having unusual decoration, and often unmarked, can pop up here and there across the country at any given time.

With many other American potteries information about experimental and very short run production pieces can be gleaned from old company records. Unfortunately, a fire at Stangl's Trenton plant in 1965 claimed the administrative area of the building, cloaking many oddities found by today's collectors in an eternal shroud of flame and ash.

This is a close-up of the mark of the quail, the entire bottom of which appears on page 61. Space was left for the model number but was never used. This mark is actually blue, the blue-green color shown here being a result of improper lighting.

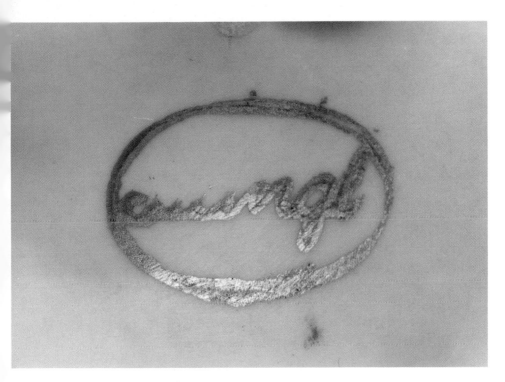

A gilted mark for a gilted bird, the Cerulean warbler shown on page 7.

The impressed mark of the grey flying duck (page 44) may be a little hard to see. It reads "Stangl / USA / 3443" on three lines.

Many Stangl birds were designed by Auguste Jacob. His signature appears on the base of one, no. 3584, the large cockatoo. The entire bird is shown on page 70.

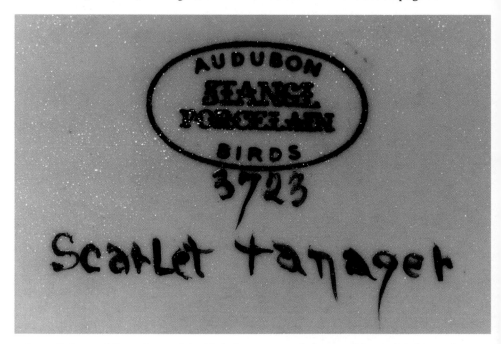

Stangl's limited line of porcelain birds incorporated the word "porcelain" into the mark so people would have no doubt about why they were so expensive. Unfortunately, it didn't seem to help much and today examples of this aborted line are extremely rare.

This paper label, or foil label if you prefer, was found on the double cockatoos, no. 3405D.

Although it's just a guess, I surmise that this paper label from the goldfinch, no. 3849, came along after the one from the double cockatoos shown above. It's simplicity not only gives it a more modern look, but possibly--perhaps most importantly--made it less expensive, too.

The paper label of the quacking duck, no. 3250 F, announces that its colonial silver finish will not tarnish, and that plain soap and water is preferable to abrasive polishes for cleaning purposes.

This is the bottom of the terra rose preening duck, no. 3250 B. Note the terra cotta clay, and the word Stangl impressed.

Originally, all Stangl birds came with a paper hang tag, most of which disappeared decades ago. Printed on both sides, this side of the label indicates the bird was made by the Stangl Pottery.

Flip the tag over and it lists the Fulper Pottery as the manufacturer of the bird. Wouldn't you love to find an indigo bunting today for the $3 price on the tag!

A Fulper paper label from the bottom of the double Audubon warblers, no. 3756D. In my opinion, this appears to be more of an inventory control sticker for company use than a paper label to identify the bird's maker to consumers.

If you are ever caught without your book and see a pair of shakers you think might be the Stangl rooster and hen, no. 3285 and 3286, the presence of a Stangl rubber stopper may confirm their identity.

Here's a real oddity--Fulper mark, Fulper clay, Fulper glaze on the Stangl running duck shown below.

It seems this 4 5/8 x 9 1/2 inch bird should have a mark identifying it as the running duck, no. 3432, in the Stangl Birds of America series. As shown above, however, it appears to be Fulper all the way. One possible explanation would be that Stangl may have recycled a Fulper artware mold for the Birds of America series. Estimated value: $500.

Chapter 3:
Stangl Values

The estimated values accompanying the pictures are not meant to set or alter prices, and should not be construed as an offer on the part of the author to buy or sell. They simply reflect what I feel a knowledgeable collector would pay a knowledgeable dealer for each bird. That statement in itself makes several assumptions. It assumes the collector can afford to pay the price for the bird. It also assumes the dealer can afford to sell it at that price, that she isn't forced to sell it lower for quick cash, or hold out for a higher price because she paid more for it than she should have.

3813 Evening Grosbeak

There are no shortcuts to valuing Stangl birds. You must familiarize yourself with each one and its value if you wish to purchase wisely, a point well illustrated by the two birds shown in this chapter, which are also shown in sequential order from different angles in Chapter 4. This one, the evening grosbeak, 4 3/4 inches high, usually goes for a little over $100. Estimated value: $130.

3923 Vermilion Flycatcher

The vermilion flycatcher is no more detailed than the evening grosbeak, and is of similar size standing 5 inches high. Consequently, you might tend to think it would sell at about the same price. Not so. It's very rare, which makes it worth several times more than the grosbeak. Estimated value: $900.

Keep in mind, too, that as you climb the Stangl bird rarity scale, which generally goes hand-in-hand with the price scale, the estimated values become less accurate. In other words, the most accurate estimated values are those of the fairly common birds costing $150 or less. These are seen and sold much more often than the rarer and more expensive ones. In the vernacular of the 90s, their commonness provides a much larger database from which to draw information. At the other end, estimated values for the rarest and highest priced birds are largely guesswork because they come on the market so seldom that virtually every time one sells, it sells for a different amount.

Sellers of Stangl birds must also consider what I like to call the satisfaction factor in regard to the higher priced birds. That means that while a very rare bird, the falcon, for example, may easily be worth its estimated value of several thousand dollars, there is probably only a handful of people in the country who would consider paying that much for it. Once that handful has been satisfied, a falcon will probably be hard to move at its true value until new collectors who desire it just as badly fill the void left by those who already possess it.

Chapter 4:
The Gallery of Stangl Birds

3250E Drinking Duck
3250D Gazing Duck
3250F Quacking Duck

The drinking duck, on the left, stands 2 inches high. Gazing duck, center, and quacking duck, right, are both 3 5/8 inches high. Estimated value: $70 each.

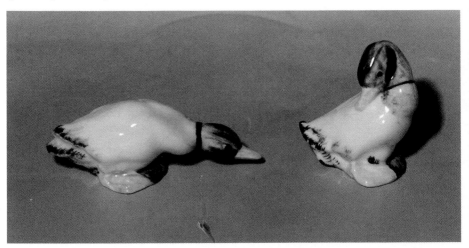

3250C Feeding Duck
3250B Preening Duck

Height of the feeding duck is 1 3/8 inches, height of the preening duck is 3 inches. Estimated value: $70 each.

3250A Standing Duck
3281 Duck

Standing duck, on the left, 3 1/4 inches high, is the sixth and final member of the above series. The duck on the right is simply called duck no. 3281. While similar in size, it is not part of the series. Height of duck no. 3281 is 3 7/8 inches. Estimated value: standing duck, $70, duck no. 3281 $125.

3250A Standing Duck

Standing duck in three different glaze treatments, green swirl, natural with brown cape, and Granada gold. Estimated value: $70 each.

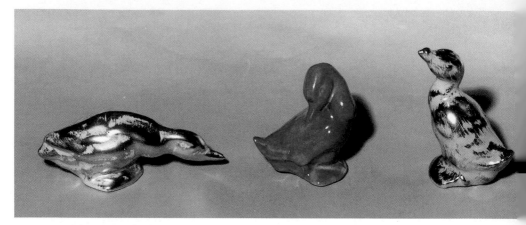

3250C Feeding Duck
3250B Preening Duck
3250F Quacking Duck

More of the 3250 series in different finishes. Left to right they are antique gold, terra rose and colonial silver. Incidentally, when ducks of the 3250 series are found with only clear (white) glaze, they go for $10-15 each. Estimated value: $70 each.

3273 Rooster

This is a fairly small bird, 5 1/2 inches high, that usually comes with a fairly high price tag. Its bottom is shown below. Estimated value: $425.

3273 Rooster

Most Stangl birds have a flat bottom with a dime- to quarter-size hole in it, but the rooster has an open bottom.

3274 Penguin

Height of the penguin is 5 1/2 inches. Estimated value: $475.

3275 Turkey

The turkey is only 3 3/8 inches high. Estimated value: $500.

3276 Bluebird
3276D Double Bluebirds

The single bluebird is 5 1/8 inches high. The double stands 8 1/4 inches. Estimated value: single $85, double $150.

3285 Roosters (originals)
3286 Hens (originals)

These are the original roosters and hens, 4 1/4 and 3 1/8 inches high, respectively. The pair on the left are figurines, the pair on the right, shakers. Bottoms are shown below. Estimated value: figurines $90 per pair, shakers $105 per pair.

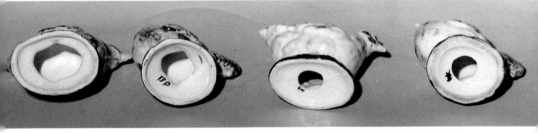

Bottoms of the above hens and roosters. Note the figurines have open bottoms, the shakers closed bottoms with holes in them.

3285 Roosters (revised)
3286 Hens (revised)

As you can see, the main difference in the revised roosters and hens is the color scheme. A more subtle difference is the sizes, 4 1/2 and 3 1/4 inches. As in the photo of the originals, the figurines are on the left, the shakers on the right. Estimated value: figurines $80 per pair, shakers $90 per pair.

3400 Lovebird (revised)
3404D Double Lovebirds (revised)

Compare these revised lovebirds to the originals on page 2 and you will notice the base of each is quite different, and that the birds of the double are not posed the same. Although the picture doesn't show it, the birds are not touching in this revised double while they are in the original. Heights are different, too, 4 3/8 and 5 1/4 for the revised examples, 4 and 4 7/8 for the originals. Estimated value: $55 single, $130 double.

3401S Wren (original)

The differences between the original and revised wrens are much more conspicuous than they are with the lovebirds. Note that the back and breast of this original single wren slant up instead of down. Height is 3 1/2 inches. Estimated value: $100.

3401S Wren (revised)

With the revised model the back and breast slant down. Besides the obvious color difference, this bird is also taller at 4 3/4 inches, and the base has been changed. As is true of the double wrens, the shape of the tail is different, as well. Estimated value: $40.

3401D Double Wrens (original)

Height of this figure is 6 1/8 inches. Estimated value: $175.

3401D Double Wrens (revised)

The height here, 6 5/8 inches, is close to that of the originals. But the color, base, attitude and tail differences make the revised double wrens unmistakable. Estimated value: $80.

3401D Double Wrens (revised)

Revised double wrens from a different angle. These measured in at 6 3/8 inches, 1/4 inch higher than the set above. Look closely and you will see the figurine is trimmed in gold. Estimated value: $125.

3402S Oriole (original)

The original oriole, 3 1/2 inches high, head pointed down, little red, simple base. Estimated value: $130.

3402S Oriole (revised)

Revised oriole, 3 1/4 inches high, head held horizontal, additional red, more detailed base. Estimated value: $50.

3402D Double Orioles (original)

Characteristics of the original double orioles, 5 5/8 inches high, are a simple base, little red, and the top bird's head is pointed down, or at the very least held horizontal. Estimated value: $150.

3402D Double Orioles (revised)

Here you see a more colorful and detailed base, the top bird with his head pointed up, and the color red is more prominent in the feathers. Height is 6 1/2 inches. Estimated value: $110.

3405 Cockatoo (small)

This cockatoo stands 6 1/8 inches high. Estimated value: $50.

3405D Double Cockatoos (original)

The original and revised double cockatoos are the same height, 9 5/8 inches. The key difference is in the base, this original pair having what is called a closed base, more fully explained in the picture at right. Estimated value: $160.

3405D Double Cockatoos (revised)

This pair of revised cockatoos was shot at approximately the same angle as the original pair . Note the large dark green leaf at lower left. If you were looking at it straight on, you would see open space between the underside of the leaf and the base, thus the reference to the open and closed base cockatoos. Estimated value: $130.

3406S Single Kingfisher

The single kingfisher in green, 3 5/8 inches high. The blue version of this bird is shown on page 3. Estimated value: blue $50, green $75.

3406D Double Kingfishers

This figurine stands 5 inches high. Estimated value: $130.

3406D Double Kingfishers

Same as above but blue-green. Estimated value: $160.

3407 Owl

The owl is a small bird not commonly found. It is 4 1/2 inches high. Estimated value: $375.

3408 Bird of Paradise (small)

The small bird of paradise stands 5 1/8 inches high. The large bird of paradise is no. 3625. Estimated value: $115.

3431 Standing Duck

The standing duck is 7 5/8 inches high. Estimated value: $475.

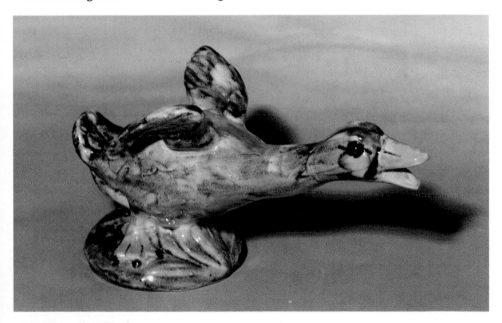

3432 Running Duck

Height of the running duck is 5 inches. An example finished in grayish white and black appears on page 8. Estimated value: $475.

3435 Rooster

This is the tallest mass produced figure in the Birds of America series, measuring a phenomenal 16 1/2 inches in height. Estimated value: $850.

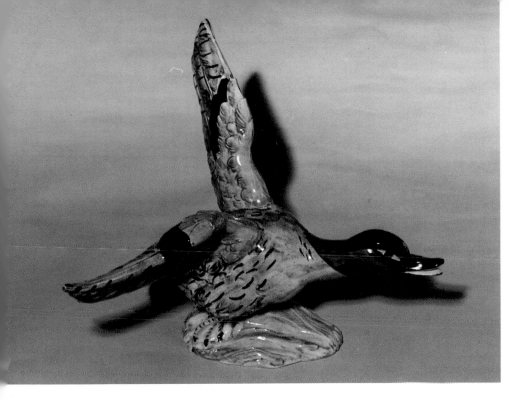

3443 Flying Duck

The flying duck is 9 inches high. This one has been finished in gray with blue on the wings. Gray examples are the most common. Estimated value: $325.

3443 Flying Duck

This one is finished in blue-green, and photographed at an angle from which you may spot it someday at an antique show. Estimated value: $400.

3443 Flying Duck

The flying duck in teal which appears to be a lighter coating of the blue-green glaze above. Estimated value: $400.

3444 Cardinal (original)

The original cardinal is 6 3/8 inches high. Identifying characteristics are a smaller crest, slimmer body and broader beak than the revised model. Estimated value: $95.

3444 Cardinal (revised)

Height of this bird is 6 1/2 inches. Estimated value: $75.

3444 Cardinal (revised)

The revised cardinal in a matte finish. It is 6 3/4 inches high. Estimated value: $125.

3445 Rooster
3446 Hen

Sizes here are exactly the same as above. Considering size, style, decoration, price etc., if I were writing an article on Stangl Birds for *Consumer Reports* I would be very tempted to list the hen and rooster as best buys. Estimated value: rooster $210, hen $175.

Opposite page, top:

3445 Rooster
3446 Hen

The hen and rooster are 7 1/2 and 9 7/8 inches high, respectively. While the rooster seems to be slightly harder to find than the hen, both are easier to come by in yellow than in the gray shown below. Estimated value: rooster $165, hen $155.

3445 Rooster

The rooster in antique gold. On this one there is a slight size difference as it measures 10 inches. Small discrepancies in size can be due to several reasons. A different slip (liquified clay poured into the mold), or an incorrectly prepared batch of slip may have been used. The kiln may have been fired hotter than it should have for one, which would make it smaller than normal, or cooler, which would make it larger. Mold growth, the process by which a mold loses detail and becomes ever so slightly larger each time it is used, may have taken place. Assume for the sake of argument that each one of these factors could alter the height of a figure 1/8 of an inch, and it becomes apparent that when working in combination with each other several different sizes could result. Estimated value: $150.

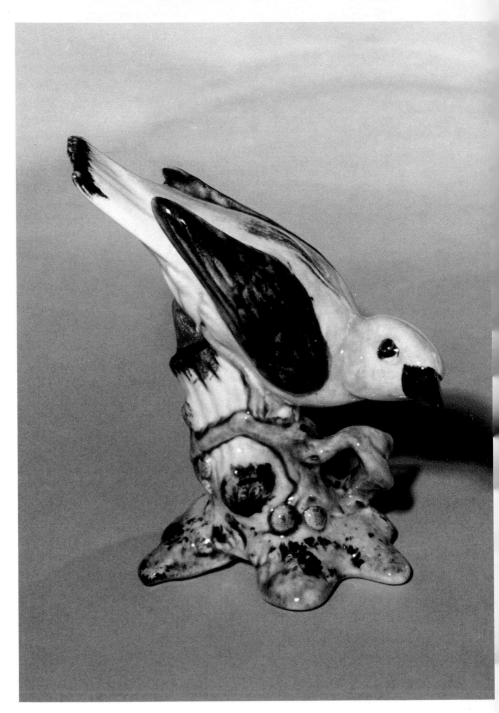

3447 Prothontary Warbler

Height of this bird, also called the yellow warbler, is 5 1/8 inches.
Estimated value: $75.

3448 Blue Headed Vireo

A 4 1/4 inch bird with a somewhat more complicated mold than many others of its size. Estimated value: $70.

3449 Paroquet (Parrot)

The parrot is 5 1/8 inches high. Estimated value: $150.

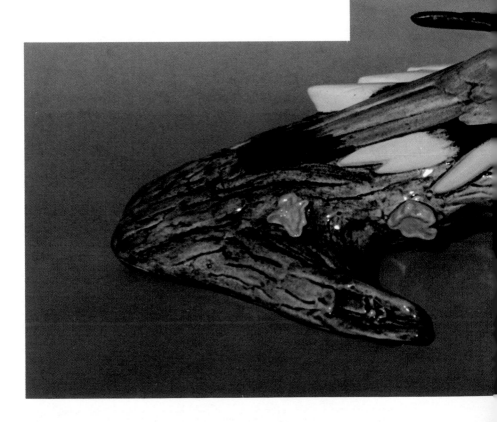

3450 Passenger Pigeon

A large figure, this bird measures 9 1/4 x 19 1/4 inches. I mentioned earlier that Stangl made some birds that Audubon never saw. Here's a case where Audubon painted a bird most of us living today have never seen. Once abundant and numbering in the millions, unbridled market hunting during the 1870s reduced the passenger pigeon population to near zero, and this beautiful species became extinct when the last one died on September 1, 1914 in the Cincinnati Zoo. Estimated value: $1000.

3451 Willow Ptarmigan

This one is 10 3/4 inches high. Note the different coloring. Estimated value: $1200.

3451 Willow Ptarmigan

The willow ptarmigan is 11 inches high. Estimated value: $1200.

3452 Painted Bunting

Height is 4 7/8 inches. Estimated value: $90.

3453 Mountain Bluebird

The mountain bluebird, 6 3/8 inches high, is a rare find. Estimated value: $600.

3454 Key West Quail Dove (one wing up)

This is a rather large bird, 9 1/2 inches high, that usually sells for a rather reasonable price. Estimated value: $225.

3454 Key West Quail Dove (wings spread)

At first glance this bird may look like it was drawn from the same mold as the one above, but it wasn't. The best place to illustrate the difference is the bird's right wing where it forms a vee with the tail. Notice how much larger the vee is on this one. This is one of those cases where the difference is blatantly obvious when you see them in person but hard to illustrate in a two-dimensional format. Also notice the additional detail on the back, wings and tail. Height is 9 inches. Estimated value: as shown, $325, in natural colors $625.

3455 Shoveler Duck

While Stangl took many artistic liberties when recreating Audubon's Birds of America, this is a case where it didn't--the drake's pose matches Audubon's print exactly. The shoveler duck is 12 5/8 inches high. It is quite rare. Estimated value: $1200.

3456 Cerulean Warbler

This Stangl bird is seen quite often. Height is 4 1/4 inches. A gilted version appears on page 7. Estimated value: $55.

3457 Pheasant

The figure measures 7 1/4 x 14 1/4 inches. This is often referred to as the walking pheasant, in contrast to the feeding pheasant. The feeding pheasant (no. 3586) is not shown. Of similar size, it was produced for the Fisher, Bruce Company, a Philadelphia distributor, and sold under the name Della Ware, which is how it is marked. You will find the feeding pheasant in color in the Duke book at the bottom of plate 1 in both natural colors and terra rose. Estimated value: $850.

3458 Quail

Rarer than the pheasant, the quail is 7 3/8 inches high. Its bottom is shown below. Estimated value: $1200.

Bottom of the quail showing stamped and impressed marks. The impressed mark, barely visible, reads "Stangl / USA" on two lines at the top of the photo, "3458" at the bottom. A close-up of the inkstamp is shown on page 12.

3459 Fish Hawk

Also called the falcon or osprey, this 10 1/4 inch high figure is generally considered to be the rarest of all the Stangl birds. Estimated value: $3000.

3490D Double Redstarts

Here are the double redstarts shown from both the front (right) and the back (left).
The pair on the left, 9 1/2 inches high, is finished the way you normally see them.
The pair on the right, 8 7/8 inches high, while less often seen is not actually what
you would consider rare. Incidentally, don't waste your time trying to obtain a
single redstart--as far as is known the company never made one. Estimated value:
left $200, right $225.

Opposite page, top:

3491 Hen Pheasant

This bird measures 6 5/8 inches in height. Its mate is shown below. Estimated value: $225.

Opposite page, bottom:

3492 Cock Pheasant

The cock pheasant is slightly shorter than the hen at 6 1/8 inches. Estimated value: $225.

3518D White-crowned Pigeons

Size of this figure is 7 7/8 x 12 1/2 inches. Duke lists them as white-headed pigeons. Estimated value: $550.

3580 Cockatoo (medium)

This is the medium cockatoo, 8 3/4 inches high. The small cockatoo is no. 3405S, the large is no. 3584. Estimated value: $130.

3580 Cockatoo (medium)

Duke describes this treatment of the medium cockatoo as ivory matte with pale yellow comb. Height is 9 inches. Estimated value: $175.

3582D Double Parakeets

Standing 7 1/4 inches high, this
same figure in blue-green is shown
on page 5. Estimated value: $230.

3581 Chickadees (group)

The chickadees measure 5 3/4 x 8 1/4 inches. The color difference is probably due to less glaze being applied to the example on the right as not only the birds, but also the branches and leaves are much paler. Estimated value: $210.

3583 Parula Warbler

This is a very common Stangl bird, often the first in many collections. It is 4 1/4 inches high. Estimated value: $45.

3584 Cockatoo (large)

The large cockatoo stands 12 1/8 inches high. It is signed "Jacob" on the lower part of the base, the signature standing for Auguste Jacob, the designer who created many of the Stangl birds. A close up of the signature is shown on page 14. Estimated value: $325.

3584 Cockatoo (large)

The large cockatoo in ivory matte with pale green comb. Height of this one is 11 1/2 inches. It is less common than the example above, and therefore somewhat more expensive. Estimated value: $400.

3585 Rufus Hummingbird
3634 Allen Hummingbird

On the right is the Rufus Hummingbird no. 3585, 3 3/8 inches high. No. 3634, the Allen Hummingbird is on the left. Height is 3 5/8 inches. Estimated value: $75 each.

3589 Indigo Bunting

Another fairly common Stangl bird, the Indigo Bunting stands 3 1/4 inches high. Estimated value: $75.

3590 Chat

Also called the Carolina wren, the chat is 4 1/2 inches high. Estimated value: $140.

3591 Brewer's Blackbird

Height here is 3 3/8 inches. Estimated value: $95.

3592 Titmouse

By no means rare, the titmouse is 3 3/8 inches high. Estimated value: $45.

3593 Nuthatch

The little nuthatch is just 2 5/8 inches high. Estimated value: $55.

3594 Red-faced Warbler

Height of the red-faced warbler is 2 3/4 inches. Estimated value: $75.

3595 Bobolink

The bobolink is 4 3/4 inches high. Estimated value: $100.

3596 Gray Cardinal

The gray cardinal is quite different than the other cardinals. It stands 5 inches high. Estimated value: $75.

3597 Wilson Warbler

This little bird is 3 inches high. Estimated value: $45.

3598 Kentucky Warbler

I have seen several of these with repaired beaks. Height is 3 5/8 inches. Estimated value: $50.

3599D Double Hummingbirds

The double hummingbirds are 8 3/4 inches high. When displayed at antique shows or in malls these often have one or more repairs. Considering the numerous projections on this figure that appear to be just waiting to be broken, one in excellent condition is a pretty good buy at the going price. Estimated value: $250.

3625 Bird of Paradise (large)

This is the large bird of paradise, 13 3/4 inches high. The small bird of paradise, no. 3408 is 5 1/8 inches high. Estimated value: $1500.

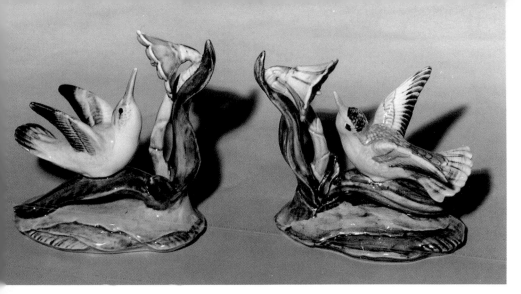

3626 Broadtail Hummingbird
3627 Rivoli Hummingbird

At first glance these two birds look exactly alike. Close scrutiny, however, will reveal several subtle differences, one of which is the broader tail of the Rivoli. The easiest way to keep them straight in your mind is the **B-B, R-R rule**, meaning that the Broadtail has a blue flower, the Rivoli a red (pink) flower. Both figures are approximately 6 1/8 inches high. Estimated value: $120 each.

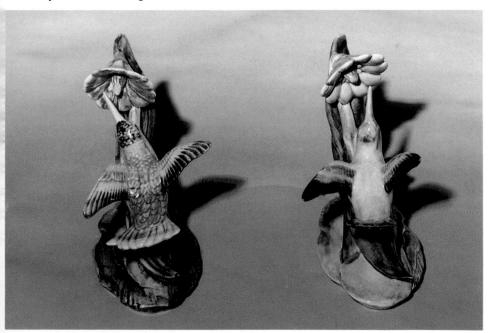

3626 Broadtail Hummingbird
3627 Rivoli Hummingbird

The Rivoli and broadtail from the end, which shows a little more about them.

3628 Riefers Hummingbird
3629 Broadbill Hummingbird

Another pair that appear to be from identical molds but really are not--note the differences in the bases and the wings. The Reifers hummingbird is on the left, the broadbill is on the right. Both are 4 7/8 inches high. Estimated value: $120 each.

3634 Allen Hummingbird: *see page 72.*

3635 Goldfinches (group)

Size of this figure is 4 1/2 x 12 1/2. It is the most common of the Stangl group figures. Estimated value: $190.

3715 Bluejay (with peanut)

The bluejay with peanut is 9 3/4 inches high, which is slightly smaller than the bluejay with leaf shown below. Estimated value: $600.

3716 Bluejay (with leaf)

The bluejay with leaf stands 10 1/2 inches high. Note that the poses of the two bluejays are not the same. Estimated value: $600.

3716 Bluejay (with leaf)

This bird displays what is called the Fulper glaze. It has a terra cotta body and a Stangl mark, but no number. Estimated value: $600.

3717D Double Bluejays

The double bluejays stand 13 inches high. They are shown from a different angle on the title page. Estimated value: $2400.

3746 Canary (facing right)
3747 Canary (facing left)

Height on the left is 6 3/8 inches. Height on the right is 6 inches. The standard factory decoration for the canary facing right was a red flower, for the canary facing left a blue flower. Estimated value: $200 each.

3749S Western Tanager
3750D Double Western Tanagers

The single figure is 5 inches high. The double figure is 8 inches high. Note the matte finish on the heads. Estimated value: single $200, double $375.

3749S Scarlet Tanager
3750D Double Scarlet Tanager

Stangl used not only the same molds for the scarlet and western tanagers, it also used the same numbers. Heights vary slightly from above, 4 1/2 and 8 1/8 inches. Estimated value: single $175, double $325.

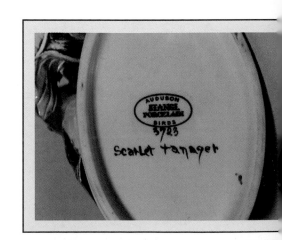

3749S Scarlet Tanager (porcelain)
3750D Double Scarlet Tanager (porcelain)

Here are the only porcelain examples shown in the book. If you ever acquire these, or any of the other Stangl porcelain birds, you will be the envy of Stangl collectors everywhere. The birds are glazed to the bases. Height of the single is 5 3/4 inches, with one-half inch of that measurement accounting for the base. The double is 7 1/8 inches high, its base being 5/8 inches thick. Estimated value of these birds has not been determined.

3749S Scarlet Tanager (porcelain)

Looking at the above photo you probably thought I was crazy calling the porcelain birds scarlet tanagers when they are finished almost exactly like the western tanagers. As you can see, I am not. But there is more. Duke shows this bird as no. 3749, which is the way I have chosen to list it even though the number on its base is clearly 3723. I have no explanation for that other than to say Mr. Duke's reputation as a competent researcher is well established, and that unless further evidence surfaces I consider the number on this example to be an anomaly.

3751S Red Headed Woodpecker (matte)

This figure, with a matte finish on its head, stands 6 1/4 inches high. Estimated value: $165.

3752D Double Red Headed Woodpecker (matte)

The double red headed woodpecker is 8 inches high. As with the single, those with the matte finish on the head are worth slightly more than those with the gloss finish shown below. Estimated value: $225.

3751S Red Headed Woodpecker (gloss)
3752D Double Red Headed Woodpecker (gloss)

Sizes here are slightly different than above, 7 3/4 inches and 6 inches. Estimated value: single $130, double $200.

3754D Double White Wing Crossbill (gloss)
3754D Double White Wing Crossbill (matte)

Both figures stand 8 5/8 inches high. No. 3754S the single white wing crossbill is not shown. The bird, of course, is very similar to those shown here. It is perched looking up on a three-footed branch base, from which another branch with one leaf extends up to about the height of the bird's beak. For a picture, see the Duke book, page 17. As far as is known, the single white wing crossbill was made only with the gloss finish. Estimated value: single $700, double (gloss) $180, double (matte) $210.

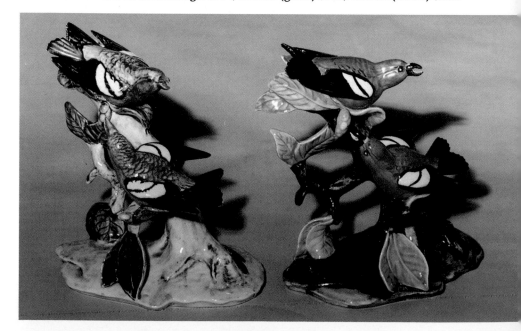

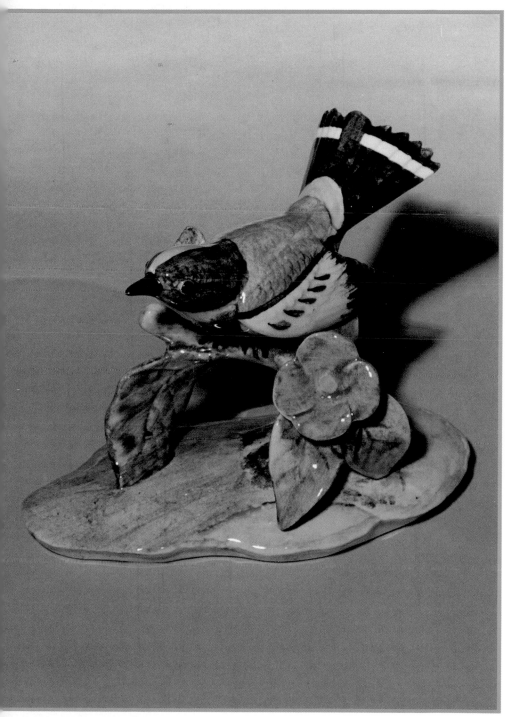

3755 Audubon Warbler

Height of this bird is 4 1/2 inches. Estimated value: $155.

3756D Double Audubon Warblers

The double Audubon warblers are 8 inches high. Note that the white band across the tail is interrupted by black, as it is with the single. Estimated value: $350.

3757 Scissortail Flycatcher

This is a tall one, 11 inches high. It is also a rather rare one. Estimated value: $650.

3758 Magpie Jay

Another fine example of a tall Stangl bird, this figure measuring 10 3/8 inches. Estimated value: $850.

3810 Black Poll Warbler

A very competently decorated black poll warbler, 3 5/8 inches high. Estimated value: $160.

3811 Chestnut Backed Chickadee

The chestnut backed chickadee is 4 7/8 inches high. Estimated value: $115.

3812 Chestnut Sided Warbler

Another bird with chestnut in its name, the chestnut sided warbler is 4 inches high. Estimated value: $90.

3813 Evening Grosbeak

The evening grosbeak is 4 3/4 inches high. Estimated value: $130.

3814 Black-throated Green Warbler

This bird has a long name but a fairly short height, 4 1/8 inches. Estimated value: $125.

3815 Western Bluebird

The western bluebird is harder to find than the [eastern] bluebird, easier to find
than the mountain bluebird. Estimated value: $400.

3848 Golden Crowned Kinglet

This figure is 4 1/8 inches high. The golden crowned kinglets group is no. 3853. Estimated value: $110.

3849 Goldfinch

The paper label of this 4-inch high goldfinch is shown close up in Chapter 2. Like other open-mouthed Stangl birds, it is often found with a repaired beak. Estimated value: $80.

3850 Yellow Warbler

The yellow warbler is 4 inches high. I haven't seen this bird a lot, so I don't know if it's the way it was made or the way I photographed it, but it sort of looks like it's wearing a saddle. Estimated value: $90.

3851 Red-breasted Nuthatch

Height of this bird is 3 5/8 inches. Estimated value: $65.

3852 Cliff Swallow

The cliff swallow stands 3 1/2 inches high. Estimated value: $125.

3853 Golden Crowned Kinglets (group)

This is the rarest of the Stangl groups. It stands 5 1/2 inches high. Estimated value: $550.

3868 Summer Tanager

Very different than the scarlet and western tanagers (no. 3749), the summer tanager is 3 7/8 inches high. Estimated value: $260.

3921 Yellow-headed Verdin

This rare bird stands 5 inches high. Estimated value: $450.

3922 European Finch

Duke shows the European finch, 4 3/4 inches high, as no. 3722. So did Joan Dworkin and Martha Horman in *A Guide to Stangl Pottery Birds*, now out of print. However, the one I photographed definitely had the number 3922 on it. Estimated value: $190.

3923 Vermillion Flycatcher

This very rare bird measures 5 3/4 inches in height. It is shown in Chapter 3 from another angle. Estimated value: $900.

3924 Yellow-throated Warbler

The yellow-throated warbler is 5 3/4 inches high. Estimated value: $175.

3925 Magnolia Warbler

The magnolia warbler, 5 1/4 inches high, is about as rare as the vermillion flycatcher above. Estimated value: $700.

Bird on Gourd Planter

Both Stangl and Pennsbury made bird on gourd planters. While Pennsbury's was its most prolific bird figural, Stangl's is probably rarer than at least half of its bird figures. The planter stands 6 3/4 inches high, is marked Stangl but does not have an identification number. Estimated value: $180.

Hen on Egg Plate

This is the hen on egg plate. The company also made a rooster on egg plate. Including the hen, the plate is 4 inches high, 9 1/4 inches in diameter. Estimated value: $75.

Opposite page:

3626 Broadtail Hummingbird Lamp

Some companies, and perhaps some individuals, too, made decorative lamps by attaching Stangl birds to stock bases. Prices run about the same as for the figurines.

3584 Large Cockatoo Lamp

A lot of bird for a small base.

3402S Revised Single Oriole Lamp

The angled shape and brushed brass of this lamp makes it look a bit more modern than the others.

3582 Double Parakeet Lamp

Background paper would have made this double parakeet lamp stand out better, but I wanted to show you how nicely it worked into this collector's decor. If you are a collector with a penchant for decorating, there is nothing to prevent you from going to a flea market, purchasing an old base and using one of your own Stangl birds to make a decorative lamp.

120

Chapter 5:
Stangl Animals

Stangl made twelve known animal figurines. Ten of them are shown here. Missing is a giraffe and a goat, both of which you can find in color in the Duke book. The animals were made about the same time that the birds went into production, the early 1940s. They apparently never caught on with the public, however, as today they are seldom seen. Few are marked. Many people who collect Stangl bird figurines also pick up the animals when and if they are lucky enough to find them.

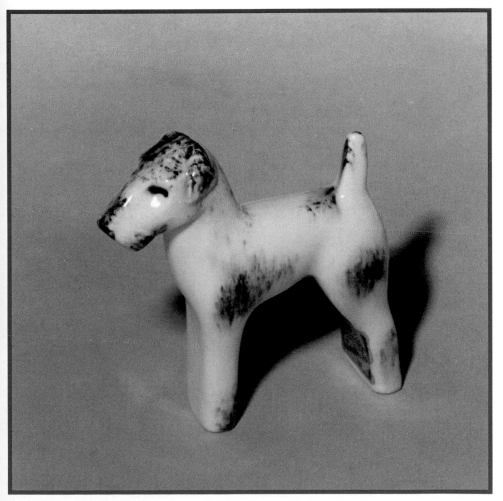

3242 Wire Haired Terrier

The wire haired terrier stands 3 1/8 inches high. Estimated value: $275.

3244 Draft Horse

All three draft horses shown here vary in size being 2 7/8, 3 1/4 and 3 1/8 inches high, left to right. Estimated values: $100 each.

3245 Rabbit
3247 Gazelle

The rabbit is 2 3/8 inches high, the gazelle 3 5/8 inches. Estimated values: rabbit $100, gazelle $100.

3246 Buffalo

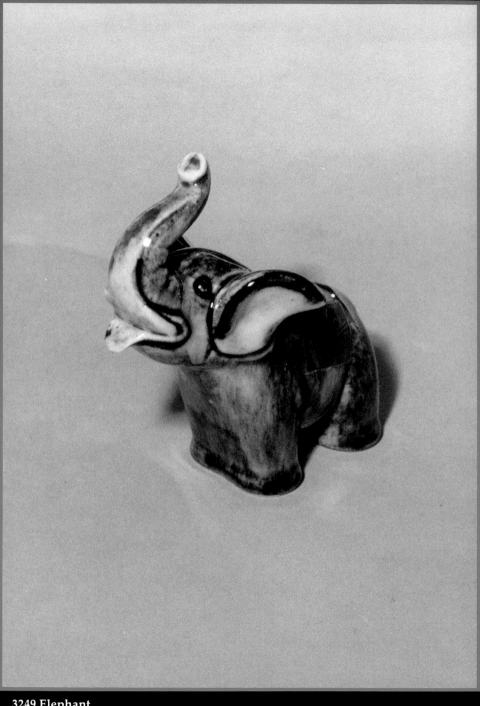

3249 Elephant

This is the smaller of the two elephants the company made. It stands 3 3/4 inches high. Note the Stangl paper label on its back. Estimated value: $125.

Elephant (number unknown)

Both of these elephants are 5 1/8 inches high. Estimated value: $55 each.

3277 Colt

The marbleized colt stands 5 1/8 inches high. Estimated value: $100 (marbleized), $275 (natural).

3280 Dog (sitting)

This is the sitting dog. It is 5 inches high, carries a Stangl mark. Estimated value: $150.

Chapter 6:
Pennsbury History

The Pennsbury Pottery made birds very similar to those produced by Stangl. It is hoped that by putting both company's birds together in one volume any confusion between the two that has existed in the past will finally be eliminated. Many aficionados of Stangl birds integrate their collections with Pennsbury birds when they run into them, as the two company's products blend together very well.

Henry and Lee Below, a husband and wife team, were former Stangl employees who, in 1950, began their own pottery in Morrisville, Pennsylvania, directly across the Delaware River from Trenton, New Jersey, the home of Stangl. They named their pottery for Pennsbury Manor, the nearby estate of William Penn, Pennsylvania's founder. Like J. Martin Stangl, the Belows came to America from Germany.

Birds were one of their first products. Overall, Pennsbury birds are rarer than Stangl birds. This is probably largely due to them being made for a much shorter time. Pennsbury birds are believed to have been a regular production item until sometime in the mid-1950s, or about five years, give or take a few. After that they were made only by special order. The company went out of business in the early 1970s. Another possible reason for their comparative rarity could be that the Pennsbury Pottery lacked the extensive marketing network of the much longer established Stangl Pottery.

Dealer Signs

As with Stangl, Pennsbury dealer signs are premium items that do not turn up very often. The signs are 4 1/4 inches high. Estimated value: $250 each.

P201 Hen
P202 Rooster

The Pennsbury Rooster is 12 inches high, the hen 10 3/4 inches. Without regard for rarity, I feel your chances of finding these at a garage sale for a couple bucks are probably better than for any of the other birds in the book. They are very light in weight. Combine that with their generally simple decoration and a person unfamiliar with them could be inclined to think they were a home ceramic or craft show item and, consequently, not worth very much money. Estimated value: $275 each.

Chapter 7:
Pennsbury Marks

Most Pennsbury birds are marked. As you can see from the pictures shown below, marks were applied freehand by decorators. As with Stangl, many include the decorator's initials for quality control purposes. A quick glance reveals that information incorporated into them was--by practice if not by policy--apparently left to the discretion of the person doing the marking. Virtually every one is different in one aspect or another. Pennsbury, however, remains the key word in each.

An exception to the nearly-always-marked rule is the gourd planters, which were seldom marked. No problem there, as gourds represent Pennsbury's most prolific bird figural and you will come to know them well in a very short time.

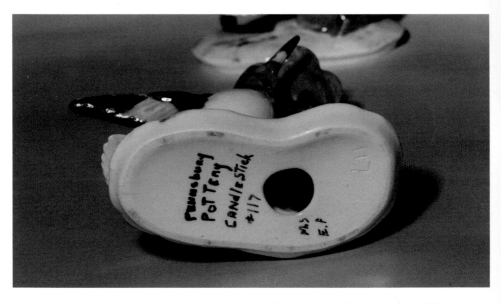

Mark of the Pennsbury candlesticks with red flower. Note the incised model number, 117, near the edge.

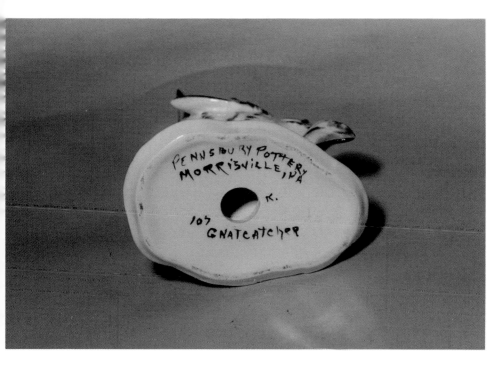

The mark of this particular gnatcatcher, no. 107, also gives the location of the pottery.

This mark on no. 101, the crested chickadee, tells when the piece was decorated.

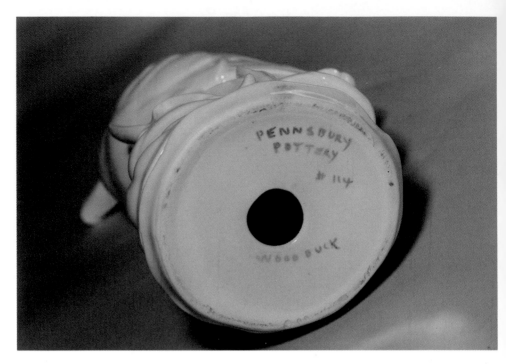

While many Pennsbury marks look pretty much alike, this one from the wood duck, no. 114, is quite different than the others.

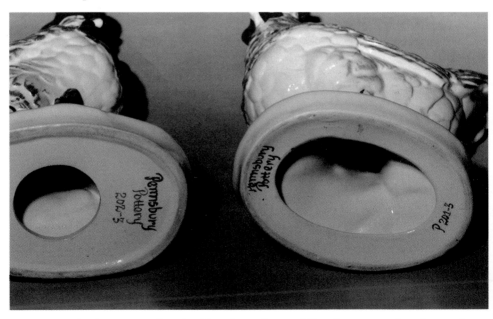

Someone had some nice handwriting for a change. More important than the marks in this picture, however, are the bottoms. Note that the rooster, on the left, was made with a closed bottom while the bottom of the hen, on the right, was pretty much open.

Chapter 8:
Pennsbury Values

The price structure of Pennsbury birds is quite different than that of Stangl birds, prices being more or less determined by size instead of by rarity. In other words, while two small Stangl birds may have vastly different values depending upon which ones they are, two small Pennsbury birds will sell for about the same price regardless of which ones they are. That statement is a generalization, of course, and assumes the quality of decoration on the Pennsbury birds to be comparable; not a decorated bird and a pure white bird, for example. In a few cases, such as that of the flying pheasant, rarity is a factor.

The price structure could change if Pennsbury birds were to become as popular as Stangl birds, and if widespread collector experience were to determine that fewer were made of certain models than of others. Given their comparative rarity, however, that event seems unlikely as there simply are not enough Pennsbury birds to support a large nationwide network of collectors.

Chapter 9:
A Gallery of Pennsbury Birds

Ring Neck Cock Pheasant (unnumbered)

This cock pheasant is highly prized. According to Henzke, pheasants were made in pairs, and by special order only. This bird is 10 1/4 inches high. Height of the hen is unknown. Estimated value: $600.

103 Bluebird

The bluebird is 3 3/4 inches high. Estimated value: $175.

102 Goldfinch

This bird has a mark similar to the mark of the crested chickadee shown in Chapter 7, "PFC Spring '65." It is 3 inches high. Estimated value: $150.

105 Scarlet Tanager
Blue-Gray Tanager (number unknown)

These birds were not measured, but according to Henzke, the scarlet tanager is 5 1/2 inches high. Tanagers were made in pairs from these two molds. Western tanagers were also produced. Estimated value: scarlet $175, blue-gray $250.

101 Crested Chickadee

The mark of this 3 3/4 inch high bird is shown in Chapter 7. Estimated value: $175.

101 Crested Chickadee

Values of undecorated (white) Pennsbury birds in this book should probably be
viewed as subjective because, in my opinion, practically any piece of mid-20th
century pottery that is undecorated is not worth nearly as much as any piece that is,
assuming that the decoration has not been botched. However, other authors such as
Lucille Henzke tend to value undecorated and decorated examples about the same.
That said, use your own best judgement when purchasing undecorated pieces.
Estimated value: $50.

119 Hummingbird
101 Crested Chickadee
103 Bluebird

The hummingbird and crested chickadee are both 4 inches high, and the bluebird is real close at 3 7/8 inches. Estimated value: hummingbird $225, crested chickadee $175, bluebird $175.

110 Nuthatch

The nuthatch is 3 1/8 inches high. Estimated value: $145.

111 Chickadee

The chickadee, 3 inches high, shown from both sides. Estimated value: $140 each.

110 Wren (small)

Pennsbury small wrens are 3 inches high. Estimated value: $120.

122 Audubon Warbler

Note the different treatment of the wings, and the color of the bases, on this Audubon Warbler and the one immediately below. Height is 4 inches. Estimated value: $225.

113 Redstart
122 Audubon Warbler
Sparrow (number unknown)

The redstart on the left is 3 3/4 inches high. The Audubon warbler is 4 inches and the sparrow 2 3/4. Estimated value: redstart $200, Audubon warbler $200, sparrow $125.

112 Magnolia Warbler

The magnolia warbler is 4 inches high. Estimated value: $200.

110 Nuthatch
Vireo (number unknown)
109 Wren (small)

Nuthatch 3 5/8 inches high, vireo 4 inches, wren 3 1/4 inches. This is the small wren. The large wren, a pedestal bird, is shown at right. Estimated value: nuthatch $150, vireo $200, small wren $120.

Opposite page:

106 Wren (large)

This is the large wren, 6 1/2 inches high. Note that not only the base is different but also the bird itself. Estimated value: $250.

144

108 Bluejay

Pennsbury's bluejay, no. 108, bears more than a slight resemblance to Stangl's. This figure is 10 1/4 inches high. Estimated value: $500.

120 Cardinal
123 Barn Swallow

The cardinal is 6 1/2 inches high. The barn swallow is just a tad shorter at 6 1/4 inches. Estimated value: cardinal $225, barn swallow $250.

120 Cardinal

Compare this cardinal to the one above and it seems Pennsbury's decorators may have been given more latitude than Stangl's decorators. Estimated value: $225.

107 Gnatcatcher

The mark of this gnatcatcher is shown in Chapter 7. Height is 7 inches. Estimated value: $250.

123 Barn Swallow

Another barn swallow, as shown above with the cardinal. Different color base, different wing and breast treatment, same price. Estimated value: $250.

123 Barn Swallow

This is what Henzke calls the late version of the barn swallow. It is 6 1/4 inches high. Estimated value: $150.

114 Wood Duck

The wood ducks are 10 1/4 inches high. When finished in natural colors they are some of Pennsbury's more desirable birds. Estimated value: white $75, natural $500.

Eagle Bookend (number unknown)

The eagle bookend stands 8 1/4 inches high. Estimated value: $150 each.

P-212 Eagle Plaque

Pennsbury made three eagle plaques. This one, P-212, is 6 1/2 inches wide. P-213 is 12 1/2 inches wide while P-214 is 22 inches. Estimated value: 6 1/2 inches $80, 12 1/2 inches $140, 22 inches $250.

Eagle (number unknown)

This is the tallest Pennsbury bird of which I am aware, standing 12 3/4 inches high. Estimated value: $550.

117 Hummingbird Candlestick
118 Hummingbird Candlestick

The hummingbird candlesticks were made in a left and right version. Here the one on the left is shown from the front, the one on the right from the back. Height is 5 inches. Estimated value: $350 per pair.

117 Hummingbird Candlestick
118 Hummingbird Candlestick

Shades of Stangl's broadtail and Rivoli hummingbirds; Pennsbury made some hummers with red flowers, others with blue. Same size as above. Estimated value: $350 per pair.

P201 Hen
P202 Rooster

The hen and rooster in Delft blue. Their heights are 12 and 10 1/2 inches. Estimated value: $375 per pair.

P201 Hen
P202 Rooster

Blue-green and slightly different sizes, 10 3/8 and 11 3/4 inches. Estimated value: $375 per pair.

P201 Hen
P202 Rooster

White and brown with red combs and wattles, 12 3/8 and 10 7/8 inches high.
Estimated value: $375 per pair.

P201 Hen
P202 Rooster

Darker brown with brown skin. Heights are 10 3/4 and 12 inches. Estimated value:
$375 per pair.

P201 Hen
P202 Rooster

Although you might think these chickens were only partially decorated, that apparently is not the case as Henzke shows a very similar set in her book. Heights are 12 and 10 3/4 inches. Estimated value: $375 per pair.

P201 Hen

This brown and yellow hen is 10 3/4 inches high. Estimated value: $190.

P201 Hen

White and green hen, not measured but within one-quarter inch of the others. Estimated value: $190.

Bird on Gourd Planter (number unknown)

The bird on gourd, called a slick chick by Henzke, is Pennsbury's most common bird figural. And this is by far the most common color scheme; those shown below are genuinely rare. Height is 5 inches. Estimated value: $45.

Bird on Gourd Planter (number unknown)

All of the Pennsbury gourds I have seen have been unmarked but Henzke shows one that is marked. As above, both of these pieces are 5 inches high. Estimated value: $125 each.

Bird on Gourd Planter (number unknown)

These two planters are even more unusual in that the birds are not solid colors. Each is 5 inches high. Estimated value: $125 each.

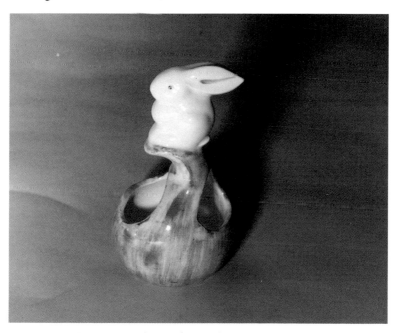

Rabbit on Gourd Planter (number unknown)

No, it's not a bird, but I bet if you are into Pennsbury birds you wouldn't pass it up. Height is 5 1/2 inches. Estimated value: $150.

Bibliography

Cox, Susan, "Investing in and Decorating with Pennsbury Pottery," *American Clay Exchange*, July 15, 1987.

----- "Pennsbury Pottery," *American Clay Exchange*, January 30, 1986

-----"Pennsbury Pottery Pictorial," *American Clay Exchange*, June 15, 1985.

----- "Stangl Birds $2.50 Each Postpaid," *American Clay Exchange*, June, 30, 1986.

Derwich, Jenny B., and Latos, Dr. Mary, *Dictionary Guide to United States Pottery & Porcelain (19th and 20th Century)*, Jenstan, Franklin, Michigan, 1984

-----"Pennsbury Pottery," *The New Glaze*, June, 1987.

Duke, Harvey, *Stangl Pottery*, Wallace-Homestead Book Company, Radnor, Pennsylvania, 1993.

Dole, Pat, "Pennsbury Pottery," *The New Glaze*, Birmingham, Alabama, April 1988.

Dworkin, Joan, and Horman, Martha, *A Guide to Stangl Pottery Birds*, Willow Pond Books, Inc., Lynbrook, New York, 1977

Evans, Paul, *Art Pottery of the United States*, Feingold & Lewis, New York, 1987.

Garth, Abe, "Stangl Items Marked," *Collector's Weekly*, July 18, 1972.

Henzke, Lucille, *Pennsbury Pottery*, Schiffer Publishing Ltd, West Chester, Pennsylvania, 1990.

-----"Stangl Audubon Birds," *The Spinning Wheel's Complete Book of Antiques*, Grosset & Dunlap, New York, 1975.

Lehner, Lois, *Lehner's U.S. Marks on Pottery, Porcelain & Clay*, Collector Books, Paducah, Kentucky, 1988

Schneider, Mike, *Animal Figures*, Schiffer Publishing Ltd., West Chester, Pennsylvania, 1990.

Stiles, Helen E., *Pottery in the United States*, E.P. Dutton & Co., New York, 1941.

Wellman, BA, "Pennsbury Pottery," *The Antique Trader Weekly*, Dubuque, Iowa, February 17, 1988.

About the author

Mike Schneider is a freelance writer whose previous works for Schiffer include *The Complete Salt and Pepper Shaker Book* and *The Complete Cookie Jar Book*, both of which have won high praise from collectors and reviewers. He is currently writing a second cookie jar book, and a series of books on California pottery, for the publisher.

Appendix 1:
Sources

Pennsbury Pottery, by Lucille Henzke, $20 plus $2.95 postage and handling. Schiffer Publishing Ltd., 77 Lower Valley Road, Atglen, PA 19310

Stangl Bird Collectors' Association. Send a check for $25 to: Stangl Bird Collectors' Association, c/o Jim Davidson, P.O. Box 419, Ringoes, NJ 08551

Stangl Pottery, by Harvey Duke, $19.95 plus $2.50 postage and handling. Stangl Book, C/O Buttzville Center, Box 106, Buttzville, NJ 07829

Appendix 2:
Stangl Porcelain Birds

In 1942 Stangl Pottery test marketed a line of twelve porcelain birds. Although the porcelain birds were exquisite in every detail, they were shunned by consumers and the experiment was short-lived. The failure was probably due to the astronomic prices for those times. The porcelain examples ran from a low of $35 for an Audubon warbler, to $250 for the double robins. By comparison, 17 years later in 1959 the catalog of Carl Forstund, Inc., of Grand Rapids, Michigan, offered five Stangl earthenware birds--oriole, wren, hummingbird, Kentucky warbler and Parula warbler--for $12.25, or $2.50 each, postpaid.

Exactly how many porcelain birds were made is unknown. Judging by how infrequently they turn up today the number must have been very small, perhaps no more than a few dozen. Guesstimates by those who are considered authorities on Stangl vary from less than ten to a couple hundred. A reasonable assumption would be that less of the larger, more complicated, higher priced porcelain figures were made than the smaller, simpler, less costly ones.

Two porcelain birds are shown in the book. The scarlet tanager and double scarlet tanager appear on page 89. All twelve are listed below in sequential order, according to Duke. Because current sales data is severely limited to nonexistent on these very rare birds, no attempt has been made to estimate their values.

3725 Red-headed woodpecker	3739 Audubon Warbler
3726 Crossbill	3740 Double Audubon warbler
3727 Double crossbill	3741 Robin
3728 Scissor-tailed flycatcher	3742 Double Robin
3729 Double red-headed woodpecker	3749 Scarlet tanager
3738 Magpie jay	3750 Double scarlet tanager

Indexes